Nebraska

by the Capstone Press
Geography Department

CAPSTONE PRESS
MANKATO, MINNESOTA

C A P S T O N E   P R E S S
818 North Willow Street • Mankato, MN 56001

Printed in the United States of America.

Library of Congress Cataloging-in-Publication Data
    Nebraska/by the Capstone Press Geography Department
    p. cm.--(One Nation)
    Includes bibliographical references and index.
    Summary: Gives an overview of the state of Nebraska, including its
    history, geography, people, and living conditions.
    ISBN 1-56065-443-0
    1. Nebraska--Juvenile literature. [1. Nebraska.]
    I. Capstone Press. Geography Dept. II. Series.
F666.3.N43 1996
978.2--dc20

                                                    96-23440
                                                      CIP
                                                       AC

Photo credits
G. Alan Nelson, cover, 8, 10, 28, 30, 36.
Nebraska Dept. of Economic Development, 4, 5, 15, 16, 25, 32.
FPG, 6, 18.
Root Resources/L.E. Schaefer, 21; Dennis MacDonald, 34;
    James Blank, 45.
James Rowan, 22, 26.

Table of Contents

Words in **boldface** type in the text are defined
in the Glossary in the back of this book.

Fast Facts about Nebraska

State Flag

Location: In the
Great Plains
region of the
Midwest
Size: 77,355
square miles
(201,123
square
kilometers)

Population: 1,578,385
(1990 United States
Census Bureau figures)
Capital: Lincoln
**Date admitted to the
Union**: March 1, 1867;
the 37th state

Western meadowlark

Largest cities: Omaha, Lincoln, Grand Island, Bellevue, Kearney, Fremont, Hastings, North Platte, Norfolk, Columbus
Nickname: The Cornhusker State
State bird: Western meadowlark

Goldenrod

State flower: Goldenrod
State tree: Cottonwood
State song: "Beautiful Nebraska" by Jim Fras and Guy Miller

Cottonwood

Chapter 1
Rodeo Days

Crowds gather on warm summer evenings in North Platte, Nebraska. They wait for the Buffalo Bill Rodeo to start. Bucking broncos push against the gates of their pens. Cowboys prepare to mount up. Suddenly, a gate opens and the first bronco bursts forth.

The cowboy waves one hand. He holds the reins in the other. Bronco riders must stay in the saddle for 10 seconds. Bull riding, calf roping, and steer wrestling also thrill this rodeo crowd.

The rodeo is part of Nebraska's history.

Buffalo Bill's ranch is a historic site in North Platte.

Buffalo Bill's Wild West Show

William Cody put together the first rodeo. It took place on July 4, 1882, in North Platte, Nebraska. About 1,000 cowboys took part.

Cody's nickname was Buffalo Bill. He had been a famous buffalo hunter and army scout. Soon, his rodeo became Buffalo Bill's Wild West Show. It toured the United States and Europe.

Today, the rodeo is part of North Platte's Nebraskaland Days. Its audiences watch a piece of Nebraska history.

Nebraska Highlights

Millions of people have crossed Nebraska since the 1800s. **Pioneers** followed the Oregon Trail west. Today, Interstate 80 runs through Nebraska. Tourists travel this highway on their way east and west.

Visitors stop at museums in Omaha. They tour the state capitol in Lincoln. Many enjoy the old towns of Kearney, Grand Island, and others. There they learn about Nebraska's history. Others like to visit the large lakes, wildlife refuges, and **fossil** beds.

Nebraskans live in a great state. Rich soil helps farmers grow large crops of corn and wheat. New industries have brought more residents to the state. Nebraska has the lowest unemployment rate of all the states. The state's high-school graduation rate is among the highest in the country.

Chapter 2

The Land

Nebraska lies in the Midwest. The state's total land area is 77,355 square miles (201,123 square kilometers). It is the 15th largest state.

The Till Plains

The Till Plains cover the eastern one-fourth of Nebraska. The state's lowest **elevation** lies in the far southeastern corner. The land there is 840 feet (252 meters) above sea level.

About 2 million years ago, glaciers moved across the plains. These sheets of ice left behind fertile soil called till. Today, farmers grow huge crops of corn and soybeans there.

The Sand Hills are in the middle of the Great Plains.

Most Nebraskans live on the Till Plains. Nebraska's largest cities, Omaha and Lincoln, are there.

The Great Plains

The Great Plains covers the rest of the state. This land gradually rises from east to west. Southwestern Kimball County has Nebraska's highest point. The land there climbs 5,426 feet (1,628 meters) above sea level.

The Sand Hills stretch across the middle of the Great Plains. Wild grasses hold the sand in place. Cattle graze on these grasses.

The Pine Ridge covers the northwestern Great Plains. Evergreen trees grow on the steep hills. Badlands are also in the Pine Ridge. Wind and rain have **eroded** the sandstone rock there. Dry riverbeds wind through these rock towers.

Rivers and Lakes

The Missouri River runs along the state's eastern border. Nebraska's other rivers flow east into the Missouri. The Platte, Niobrara, and Republican are major Nebraska rivers.

Most of Nebraska's 2,000 lakes are small. Many of them dot the Sand Hills. Nebraska's largest lakes were made by damming rivers. Lake McConaughy is the largest of these. It is on the Platte River.

Climate

Nebraska can be very hot in the summer. Temperatures are often 100 degrees Fahrenheit

(38 degrees Celsius). Winter days can be very cold. The temperature can fall below 0 degrees Fahrenheit (minus 18 degrees Celsuis).

Eastern Nebraska gets the most rain and snow each year. Western Nebraska is the driest part of the state. Only about 15 inches (38 centimeters) of rain and snow fall there.

Storms hit Nebraska throughout the year. Blizzards blow snow across Nebraska. Thunderstorms and tornadoes cross the state in the spring. Hailstorms can damage crops. Sudden heavy rainstorms sometimes flood shallow creeks and riverbeds.

Wildlife

Nebraska has interesting wildlife. Prairie dogs live in underground tunnels on the Great Plains. Antelope and elk graze in the Pine Ridge. Bison live in wildlife refuges in western Nebraska.

Quail, partridge, and pheasants live along the state's rivers. Sandhill cranes flock to the Platte River each spring.

Elk graze in the Pine Ridge area of Nebraska.

Chapter 3
The People

Almost 94 percent of Nebraskans are white. Their **ancestors** came to Nebraska after a treaty opened the area to settlement in 1854. Thousands arrived from states to the east. Many others came from Europe. These settlers farmed the land. They built hundreds of small towns.

Many Nebraskans still live on farms or in small towns. However, 66 percent of Nebraskans live in large towns and cities.

European Ethnic Groups

Nebraska's European settlers came from many different countries. Large numbers came

The town of Wilber calls itself the Czech capital of Nebraska.

Nebraska's most famous African American is Malcolm X.

from Germany, Ireland, Norway, Sweden, Denmark, and Bohemia. They arrived by train or covered wagon.

Most of the Europeans were farmers. Many others helped lay railroad tracks through Nebraska. Others built towns along the Missouri and Platte rivers.

The **immigrants** named some towns after places in Europe. Danish people settled Danneborg. Swedish families founded Stromsburg.

Some communities still have strong ties to a single country. O'Neill is an Irish town in central Nebraska. St. Patrick's Day lasts three days there. The town of Wilber calls itself the Czech capital of Nebraska.

African Americans

African Americans have lived in Nebraska since the 1850s. They claimed homesteads and built farms. Other African Americans worked as cowboys.

More African Americans came to Nebraska after World War II (1939-1945). They found jobs in Nebraska's industries.

African Americans now make up 3.6 percent of the population. Most of them live in Lincoln or Omaha.

Nebraska's most famous African American is Malcolm X. He was born in Omaha in 1925.

Hispanic Americans

Nebraska's Hispanic population totals only 2.3 percent. That is about 37,000 people. Hispanic Americans have Spanish-speaking ancestors. Many of their families came from Mexico.

Some Hispanics live in Nebraska only during the harvest season. They work on the state's farms.

Hispanics in Scottsbluff hold celebrations in May and September. Mexican food and dances are part of these festivals.

Native Americans

Many Native Americans once lived in Nebraska. They lost their land to white settlers in the 1800s. Most Native Americans were forced onto **reservations** by 1890.

Today, three tribes live on reservations in Nebraska. The Santee Sioux, Omaha, and Winnebago reservations are in eastern Nebraska. Other Sioux live in the northwestern Pine Ridge area. About 12,500 Native Americans live in Nebraska.

Each tribe hosts its own powwow every summer. Tribal members wear traditional costumes. The Winnebago perform a Medicine

Scottsbluff is home to many Hispanics.

Dance. They also sell woven baskets. The Omaha powwow may be one of North America's oldest festivals.

Asian Americans

About 12,500 Asian Americans live in Nebraska. Many of their families came from China, Korea, and Vietnam.

Chapter 4
Nebraska History

Nebraska's first people arrived about 12,000 years ago. They hunted early kinds of bison.

Ancestors of today's Native Americans moved into Nebraska thousands of years later. The Pawnee, Oto, and Omaha built villages. They raised corn, beans, and squash. The Sioux, Cheyenne, Arapaho, and Comanche roamed the Great Plains. They became great buffalo hunters.

European Explorers and Traders

Spain and France had claimed parts of western North America by the late 1600s. Both countries claimed Nebraska. Spanish soldiers

Native Americans roamed the Great Plains for many years.

tried to push the French from Nebraska in the early 1700s. Native Americans defeated the Spaniards.

French explorers and traders traveled along the Missouri and Platte rivers. The traders exchanged goods with Native Americans. They traded beads and kettles for beaver pelts and deer hides.

Americans in Nebraska

The United States became a country in 1776. Nebraska was far to the west of this new country.

France sold its North American land in 1803. The United States bought it. American explorers and traders traveled through Nebraska. Robert Stuart blazed a trail along the Platte River in 1813. It connected the Great Plains to Oregon. This was the Oregon Trail.

During the 1840s, thousands of settlers traveled the Oregon Trail. They could not stay in Nebraska, however. The United States government had set Nebraska aside as Indian territory.

During the 1840s, thousands traveled the Oregon Trail.

Statehood

The government opened Nebraska to settlers in 1854. Farmers settled in the Platte and Missouri valleys. Bellevue, Omaha, and Grand Island were founded by 1857.

The Homestead Act of 1862 brought many new settlers. **Homesteaders** got 160 acres (64 hectares) of land. They were to live on and

work the land for five years. Then the land was theirs.

Nebraska soon had enough people to become a state. In 1867, Nebraska became the 37th state. Lincoln became the new state's capital.

Farming the Land

Many early farmers had a hard time. Grasshoppers ate their crops in the 1870s. Crops died in the **drought** of 1890. Hardly any rain fell that year.

Nebraska farmers started to **irrigate** their fields by the 1900s. Engineers built dams along the Platte River. The dams created **reservoirs** of water. Farmers used this water to irrigate their fields. Irrigation helped their crops live through the long, dry summers.

Ranchers began using northwestern Nebraska as cattle country. This land was not good for farming. Its grasses were perfect for grazing cattle, however.

Nebraska's land is perfect for grazing cattle.

The Platte River was used for crop irrigation.

The Great Depression and World War II

The Great Depression hit the United States in 1929. Many workers lost their jobs. Prices for farm crops fell. Droughts in the 1930s turned the land to dust. Strong winds made Nebraska part of the Dust Bowl. Many Nebraskans lost their farms. More than 60,000 people left the state.

Better times started again in the 1940s. Good rainfalls helped Nebraskans grow big crops. Prices for farm goods rose.

The United States entered World War II in 1941. Nebraska grew corn and wheat for the soldiers. Meat-packing plants and transportation businesses grew in the cities.

Recent Changes

The state's economy changed in the 1960s and 1970s. Many **rural** people sold their family farms. Agricultural companies bought these small farms. Service businesses in Omaha and Lincoln hired new workers. Thousands of people moved to Nebraska for these jobs.

Nebraska worked to bring in new industries in the 1980s. The state had a healthy economy by the 1990s. Nebraska's economy includes farming, industry, and service businesses.

Chapter 5
Nebraska Business

Nebraska has the lowest unemployment rate in the nation. New businesses help keep unemployment down. Agriculture is still important to the state. Many Nebraska businesses rely on a good harvest.

Agriculture

Nebraska farms cover about 95 percent of the state. That is the largest percentage of farmland of all the states. Huge cornfields cover eastern Nebraska. Wheat is more common in the west. Soybeans, **sorghum**, and hay are other Nebraska crops.

Cornfields are a common sight in eastern Nebraska.

Many tourists visit the Stuhr Museum in Grand Island.

Ranching is important in the Sand Hills region. Cattle graze on the grassy dunes. Farmers throughout the state raise sheep, hogs, turkeys, and chickens. Nebraska beekeepers produce honey.

Manufacturing

More than 100,000 people have manufacturing jobs. Many of them work in food-processing companies. Breakfast cereals, bread, and livestock feed are important products. Omaha, Grand Island, and Fremont have large meat-packing plants. Other companies make milk products and soft drinks.

Farm machinery is another important product. Electrical and telephone equipment are also made in the state.

Government Work

Nebraska has about 150,000 government workers. Many work at Offutt Air Force Base. Others have jobs on Nebraska's three Indian reservations.

Service Industries

Service industries are Nebraska's biggest moneymakers. They employ almost 60 percent of the state's workers.

Service industries include insurance and tourism. Mutual of Omaha is the largest private insurance company in the nation. Tourists spend almost $2 billion a year in Nebraska. They visit the state's cities, historical sites, and wildlife refuges.

Chapter 6

Seeing the Sights

Nebraska is a huge state. It has many great places to visit. Many pioneer landmarks, forts, and homes have been restored. Nebraska's cities have museums and zoos. Tourists and Nebraskans enjoy the state's rivers, lakes, and prairies.

Missouri River Country

The Missouri River forms Nebraska's eastern border. Fort Atkinson was the first fort built west of the river. Visitors can see old dishes and uniforms from the 1820s.

Omaha is south of the fort. It is Nebraska's largest city. The Great Plains Black Museum is there. It tells the story of African Americans on the frontier. The Joslyn Art Museum shows many Western paintings and sculptures. The Henry Doorly Zoo has more than 2,500 animals.

The State Capitol in Lincoln is a popular site.

Fort Kearney was a post on the Oregon Trail.

Boys Town is in Omaha. Father Edward Flanagan founded this home for abandoned boys in 1917. Now more than 500 boys and girls live there.

The Strategic Air Command Museum is south of Omaha, near Bellevue. The museum displays many aircraft and missiles. It is at Offutt Air Force Base.

Bellevue was the first settlement in Nebraska. The state's first church still stands there.

The state capital at Lincoln is to the southwest. The tower of the capitol building is 400 feet (120 meters) high. Lincoln also is home to the University of Nebraska. The Cornhuskers play football there.

Towns Along the Platte River

The Platte River cuts through the center of Nebraska. Grand Island is the largest city on the Platte. Visitors enjoy the Stuhr Museum of the Prairie Pioneer. A bank, schoolhouse, hotel, and blacksmith shop are part of the museum.

Kearney is west of Grand Island. It was named for Fort Kearney. This was a post on the Oregon Trail. The fort's blacksmith shop and stockade have been restored. Today, visitors camp, hike, and fish at the fort's park.

North Platte is west of the fort. The North Platte and South Platte rivers come together there. Buffalo Bill Cody built Scout's Rest Ranch in North Platte. Visitors can tour the 18-room home and see buffalo grazing.

Scenery Along the North Platte River

Lake McConaughy lies farther west along the North Platte River. A dam on the North Platte formed this lake. It is the largest lake in Nebraska. The lake is used for boating, fishing, and swimming.

Bridgeport is still farther west. Visitors there can take a covered-wagon trip over part of the Oregon Trail. Travelers on the trail can see Chimney Rock. It rises almost 500 feet (150 meters).

Scotts Bluff National Monument is to the northwest. This 800-foot (240-meter) bluff was another landmark on the Oregon Trail. Today, visitors can drive or hike to the bluff's top.

Sand Hills Region

Valentine is in far northern Nebraska. The Sandhills Museum is there. This museum shows tools used by early cattle ranchers.

The Fort Niobrara National Wildlife Refuge is north of Valentine. Buffalo, elk, and longhorn cattle graze there.

Pine Ridge Region

Pine forests and rocky **buttes** cover northwestern Nebraska. The town of Alliance is in southern Pine

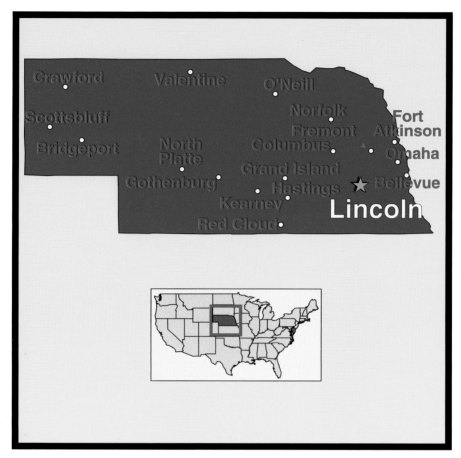

Ridge. Outside the town is Carhenge. This is a circle of cars standing on end.

Fort Robinson State Park is to the north. The United States Army fought the Plains Indians there. The fort now offers stagecoach rides and cookouts.

Agate Fossil Beds National Monument is southwest of the fort. Visitors can see fossils of prehistoric animals. Some are more than 19 million years old.

Nebraska Time Line

10,000 B.C.—Early people arrive in Nebraska.

1541—Spain claims land that includes Nebraska.

1682—France claims land that includes Nebraska.

1714—Etienne Veniard de Bourgmont explores Nebraska's Missouri River valley.

1720—Native Americans attack and defeat Spanish forces in Nebraska.

1739—The Mallet brothers cross Nebraska along the Platte River.

1803—France sells its North American land, including Nebraska, to the United States.

1819—The United States Army builds Fort Atkinson on the west bank of the Missouri River.

1823—Nebraska's first white settlement is built at Bellevue.

1840s—Settlers heading west follow the Oregon Trail along the Platte River.

1854—The Kansas-Nebraska Act creates the Nebraska Territory.

1862—The Homestead Act attracts more settlers to Nebraska.

1867—Nebraska becomes the 37th state.

1879—Fighting between Indians and the United States Army in Nebraska ends.

1902—The United States government sets aside money for irrigation projects in Nebraska.

1917—Father Edward Flanagan begins what becomes Boys Town.

1930s—Dust storms destroy topsoil and crops throughout Nebraska.

1934—Nebraska establishes a unicameral (one-house) legislature.

1946—The Strategic Air Command builds its headquarters in Nebraska.

1955—Omaha becomes the country's major livestock center.

1970—Interstate 80 is completed through Nebraska.

1974—Gerald Ford, born in Omaha, becomes president of the United States.

1986—Kay Orr becomes the first woman elected as governor of Nebraska.

1994—Nebraska's farms produce record corn and soybean crops.

Famous Nebraskans

Grace Abbott (1878-1939) Social worker who worked to improve the lives of children and their mothers; helped write the Social Security Act; born in Grand Island.

Fred Astaire (1899-1987) Movie star known for his graceful dancing style; born in Omaha.

Marlon Brando (1924-) Movie star who won Academy Awards for best actor for his roles in *On the Waterfront* and *The Godfather*; born in Omaha.

William Jennings Bryan (1860-1925) Lawyer and politician who worked for farm reforms; ran for the president of the United States and lost three times; lived in Lincoln.

Willa Cather (1873-1947) Writer whose novels *O Pioneers!* and *My Antonia* describe Nebraska pioneer life; lived in Red Cloud.

Henry Fonda (1905-1982) Movie star who won the Academy Award for best actor for his role in *On Golden Pond*; born in Grand Island.

Bob Gibson (1935-) Baseball pitcher who won 20 games in each of five seasons; named to the Baseball Hall of Fame; born in Omaha.

Malcolm X (1925-1965) Author and activist for the rights of African Americans; born in Omaha.

Julius Sterling Morton (1832-1902) Early Nebraska settler who started the idea of Arbor Day; lived in Nebraska City.

Susan LaFlesche Picotte (1865-1915) Omaha Indian who became the first Native American to earn a medical degree; born in Omaha.

Red Cloud (1822-1909) Oglala Sioux chief who defeated United States troops during campaigns in Nebraska, Wyoming, and Montana; born in Nebraska.

Marie Sandoz (1896-1966) Writer whose books told of life in western Nebraska; *Love Song to the Plains* is a history of Nebraska; born in Sheridan County.

Glossary

ancestor—a person from whom someone is descended, such as a grandmother or a great-grandfather

butte—hill that rises sharply from the surrounding area and has a flat top

drought—long period of little or no rainfall

elevation—the height of land in relation to sea level

erode—the wearing away of land

fossil—the remains or imprint of ancient plants or animals preserved in the earth's crust

homesteader—a settler who obtained land by paying a small fee and then lived on and improved the land for a set number of years

immigrant—one who comes to another country to settle

irrigate—a system of bringing water to fields and crops

pioneer—the first people who come into an area

reservation—land set aside for Native Americans

reservoir—lake or pond where water is collected and stored

rural—relating to the country

sorghum—a grain crop used in livestock feed

The Joslyn Art Museum in Omaha shows Western paintings and sculptures.

To Learn More

Hargrove, Jim. *Nebraska*, America the Beautiful series. Chicago: Children's Press, 1989.

Porter, A. P. *Nebraska*. Minneapolis: Lerner Publications, 1991.

Robison, Nancy. *Buffalo Bill*. New York: Franklin Watts, 1991.

Welsch, Roger L. *It's Not the End of the Earth, But You Can See It from Here: Tales of the Great Plains*. New York: Villard Books, Inc., 1990.

Internet Sites

City.Net Nebraska
http://www.city.net/countries.united_states/nebraska
Travel.org-Nebraska
http://.travel.org/nebraska.html
Nebraska State Government
http://www.state.ne.us/
Nebraska Tourism and Travel
http://www.ded.state.ne.us/tourism.html

Useful Addresses

Agate Fossil Beds National Monument
P.O. Box 27
Gering, NE 69341

Boys Town
13603 Flanagan Boulevard
Boys Town, NE 68010

Buffalo Bill Ranch State Historical Park
Buffalo Bill Avenue
North Platte, NE 69101

Strategic Air Command Museum
2510 SAC Place
Bellevue, NE 68005
E-mail: SACMuseum@aol.com

Stuhr Museum of the Prairie Pioneer
3133 West Highway 34
Grand Island, NE 68801

Willa Cather Historical Center
326 North Webster Street
Red Cloud, NE 68970

Index